Dear Parent:
Your child's love of reading starts here!

Every child learns to read in a different way and at his or her own speed. Some go back and forth between reading levels and read favorite books again and again. Others read through each level in order. You can help your young reader improve and become more confident by encouraging his or her own interests and abilities. From books your child reads with you to the first books he or she reads alone, there are I Can Read Books for every stage of reading:

SHARED READING
Basic language, word repetition, and whimsical illustrations, ideal for sharing with your emergent reader

BEGINNING READING
Short sentences, familiar words, and simple concepts for children eager to read on their own

READING WITH HELP
Engaging stories, longer sentences, and language play for developing readers

READING ALONE
Complex plots, challenging vocabulary, and high-interest topics for the independent reader

ADVANCED READING
Short paragraphs, chapters, and exciting themes for the perfect bridge to chapter books

I Can Read Books have introduced children to the joy of reading since 1957. Featuring award-winning authors and illustrators and a fabulous cast of beloved characters, I Can Read Books set the standard for beginning readers.

A lifetime of discovery begins with the magical words **"I Can Read!"**

Visit www.icanread.com for information
on enriching your child's reading experience.

Special thanks to teachers Gina Ludlow and Cynthia Hill
—S.A.

I dedicate this book to Sasha, who inspires me daily
—C.K.

Picture Credits

The following photograph is courtesy of Christine King Farris & King Estate: page 26, family portrait of the Kings taken in 1939. Copyright © 1939 by Dr. Martin Luther King Jr., © renewed 1967 by Coretta Scott King.

The following photograph is courtesy of the Library of Congress: page 31, protest march from Selma to Montgomery, Alabama—Photographer Peter Pettus.

The following photographs are © Getty Images: page 26, Rosa Parks, Underwood Archives; page 27, Dr. King leading peace march in Washington—Photographer Hulton Deutsch; Dr. King getting the Nobel Peace Prize, Keystone; page 28, Yolanda King as a baby, Michael Ochs Archives; the King family at the piano—Photographer Donald Uhrbrock; page 29, Martin Luther III playing baseball, Flip Schulke Archives; Sunday dinner prayer, Flip Schulke Archives; page 30, carpooling during the bus boycott—Photographer Don Cravens; lunch counter protest, Bettmann; page 31, Dr. King leading the march in Washington—Photographer Robert W. Kelley; escorting African American children to newly integrated school, Bettmann; Dr. King in jail, Bettmann; page 32, Dr. King at the Prayer Pilgrimage, Hulton Archive.

I Can Read Book® is a trademark of HarperCollins Publishers.

Library of Congress Control Number: 2017943574
ISBN 978-0-06-243276-6 (trade bdg.)—ISBN 978-0-06-243275-9 (pbk.)

Book design by Jeff Shake

17 18 19 20 LSCC 10 9 8 7 6 5 4 3 2

❖   First Edition

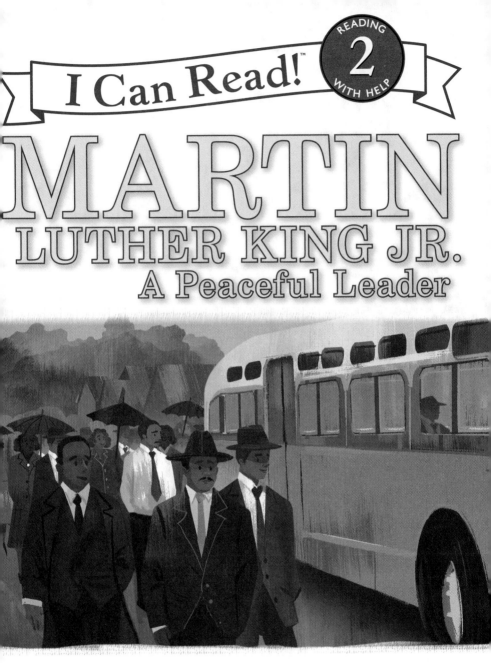

I Can Read!

READING 2 WITH HELP

MARTIN LUTHER KING JR.
A Peaceful Leader

by Sarah Albee
pictures by Chin Ko

HARPER
An Imprint of HarperCollinsPublishers

Martin Luther King Jr.

was born in 1929.

He and his family lived

in a pretty yellow house

in Atlanta, Georgia.

His father was a minister.

There were lots of books at home.
Young Martin was a happy child.
But as he grew older, he realized
that black people and white people
were not treated the same way.

Once, Martin's father took him
to buy new shoes.
The white salesman asked them
to move to the back of the store.
They left.

Another time, Martin accidentally
stepped on a white lady's toe.
She slapped him
and called him a bad name.
He did not react with anger.
He believed that bravery meant
peacefully standing your ground.

At home Martin learned to listen,
ask questions, and speak up.
He finished high school
in just two years.
He went to college at age fifteen.

Then he continued his studies.

Should he be a lawyer? A doctor?

Perhaps a professor?

Martin chose to become a minister,

like his father and grandfather.

He earned his PhD, and became

Dr. Martin Luther King Jr.

In the United States in the 1950s,
black people and white people
were still not treated as equals.
Separating black people
and white people
was known as segregation.

In some states,
there were separate—and not as nice—
bathrooms, playgrounds,
and schools for black people.
Black people had to give up
their bus seats for
white passengers.

Dr. King and his new wife, Coretta,

moved to Montgomery, Alabama.

He had a job as a pastor at a church.

His words were powerful.

He was a natural leader.

He joined the civil rights movement.

Other black leaders were impressed
by the young preacher.
They thought he would be
a good person to help
lead their cause.

Then a moment came where Dr. King
felt he could make a difference.
A woman named Rosa Parks
refused to give up her seat on a bus.
She was arrested.
This was in 1955.
It happened in Montgomery.

Dr. King and other civil rights leaders organized a protest. Dr. King urged black people to stop riding the city's buses.

For 381 days,

most black people

stopped riding buses to work.

They walked and carpooled.

Dr. King walked with them.

The protest worked.

The Supreme Court ruled

that buses in Montgomery

would no longer be segregated.

Dr. King helped change the law.

He had changed it peacefully.

Under Dr. King's leadership,
the civil rights movement grew.
Black people bravely sat down
in "whites-only" restaurants.
Black children bravely attended
"whites-only" schools.

Black people and white people marched together.
They kept protesting unfair laws, and they did it peacefully.

Some people were afraid
of what would happen
if laws were changed.
Some were so angry they shouted,
set fires, and beat protesters.
Once, a bomb went off
on Dr. King's porch.

Dr. King and other leaders
were arrested many times.
Dr. King showed everyone
how to stand up for what is right.
Peaceful protest took courage.

In 1963, thousands of people
marched in Washington, DC.
Dr. King gave a powerful speech.
The world watched him on TV.
In 1964, Dr. King won the
Nobel Peace Prize, a reward
for his work to create fairness
without violence.

Then one day in 1968,
a white man shot Dr. King.
Dr. King died the next day.
Millions mourned him.

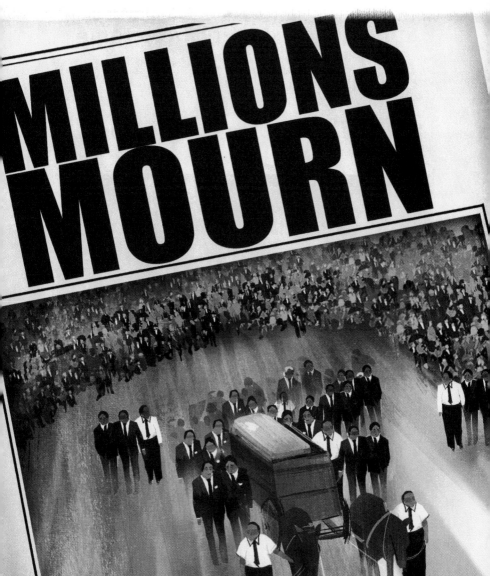

Dr. King had known he might not live
to see liberty and justice for all.
But he believed there were things
worth dying for.
Dr. King's courage and his love,
his ability to lead and to be heard,
would live on.
In his short lifetime,
Dr. King changed the way
people saw one another.

Timeline

1929

Martin Luther King Jr. is born in Atlanta, Georgia. Martin is ten in this family photo.

1948

King graduates from Morehouse College.

1953

King marries Coretta Scott.

1955

Rosa Parks is arrested for refusing to give up her bus seat.

1920

1930

1940

1950

1960

Timeline (continued)

1963
Dr. King leads a peace march in Washington, DC, and delivers a speech that millions of people would remember.

1964
Dr. King receives the Nobel Peace Prize.

1964
The Civil Rights Act is passed, making it illegal to treat people unfairly.

1968
Dr. King is assassinated.

1983
The third Monday of January becomes Martin Luther King Jr. Day, a national holiday.

Martin Luther King Jr. and His Young Family

Martin Luther King Jr. and Coretta Scott married in 1953. They had four children. Yolanda was born in 1955, Martin Luther III (Marty) in 1957, Dexter in 1961, and Bernice in 1963.

Here are Martin and Coretta with Yolanda.

Coretta Scott King had earned a degree in voice and violin from a famous music school.

After her husband's death, she spent much of her life working for peace and justice.

Here's Martin throwing a ball to Marty (Martin Luther III).

The family prays before eating Sunday dinner. There's a picture of Gandhi over the doorway. Mahatma Gandhi was a leader from India who believed in peaceful protest. Dr. King admired him greatly.

Peaceful Protest

Like his hero, Gandhi, Dr. King led peaceful protests. It wasn't easy. He was arrested thirty times. Protests included marches, boycotting buses, sitting down at "whites-only" lunch counters in restaurants, and helping black children go to formerly "whites-only" schools.

Carpooling during the bus boycott in Montgomery, Alabama.

African American students sitting at a lunch counter to protest segregation.

Martin Luther King Jr. and other leaders march in Washington, DC, in 1963.

The civil rights protest march from Selma to Montgomery, Alabama, in 1965.

Martin Luther King Jr. and other leaders escorting African American children to their newly integrated school in Mississippi.

Dr. King in jail, in 1967.

Through powerful words and peaceful actions, Dr. King
became America's greatest champion of fairness and
justice for all.